KANSAS

The Sunflower State

BY
JOHN HAMILTON

Abdo & Daughters

An imprint of Abdo Publishing | abdopublishing.com

abdopublishing.com

Published by ABDO Publishing, a division of ABDO, PO Box 398166, Minneapolis, Minnesota 55439. Copyright © 2017 by Abdo Consulting Group, Inc. International copyrights reserved in all countries. No part of this book may be reproduced in any form without written permission from the publisher. ABDO & Daughters™ is a trademark and logo of ABDO Publishing.

Printed in the United States of America, North Mankato, Minnesota.
012016
092016

Editor: Sue Hamilton   **Contributing Editor:** Bridget O'Brien
Graphic Design: Sue Hamilton
Cover Art Direction: Candice Keimig   **Cover Photo Selection:** Neil Klinepier
Cover Photo: iStock
Interior Images: Alamy, AP, Charles Conlon, Corbis, Dreamstime, FC Kansas City, Getty, Granger, History in Full Color-Restoration/Colorization, Ian McMurtry, iStock, John Hamilton, Kansas City T-Bones, Kansas State Historical Society, Kansas Turnpike Authority, Library of Congress, Mile High Maps, Minden, NASA, NOAA, Richard Hambrick, Schlitterbahn Waterpark, Sporting Kansas City, University of Kansas, Wichita Thunder, Wichita Wingnuts, & Wikimedia.

Statistics: *State and City Populations*, U.S. Census Bureau, July 1, 2014 estimates; *Land and Water Area*, U.S. Census Bureau, 2010 Census, MAF/TIGER database; *State Temperature Extremes*, NOAA National Climatic Data Center; *Climatology and Average Annual Precipitation*, NOAA National Climatic Data Center, 1980-2015 statewide averages; *State Highest and Lowest Points*, NOAA National Geodetic Survey.

Websites: To learn more about the United States, visit booklinks.abdopublishing.com. These links are routinely monitored and updated to provide the most current information available.

Cataloging-in-Publication Data

Names: Hamilton, John, 1959- author.
Title: Kansas / by John Hamilton.
Description: Minneapolis, MN : Abdo Publishing, [2017] | Series: The United
    States of America | Includes index.
Identifiers: LCCN 2015957605 | ISBN 9781680763186 (lib. bdg.) |
    ISBN 9781680774221 (ebook)
Subjects: LCSH: Kansas--Juvenile literature.
Classification: DDC 978.1--dc23
LC record available at http://lccn.loc.gov/2015957605

CONTENTS

THE SUNFLOWER STATE

Some say Kansas is in the middle of nowhere and flat as a pancake. But those people don't know the real Kansas. Yes, there are wide-open spaces, including endless fields of wheat, corn, and sorghum. Kansas farmers help feed the nation. But the state also has forests, rivers, weird rock formations, and marshes. The Flint Hills rise up in the east. And even though Kansas is far from Hollywood or Broadway, the state has a rich cultural life. Kansans love the arts, especially music and literature.

In 1939, *The Wizard of Oz* portrayed Kansas as a land filled with simple farm folk. Today, farmers still work the land, but the state is also home to aircraft engineers, teachers, biologists, and energy scientists.

Kansas is nicknamed "The Sunflower State" as a reminder of its prairie heritage. Colorful wild sunflowers are still found all over Kansas. There is even a sunflower on the Kansas state flag.

Many businesses are found in modern Wichita, Kansas.

QUICK FACTS

KANSAS

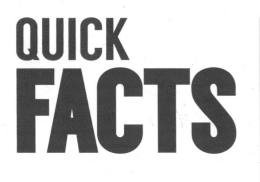

Name: Kansas is named after a Native American tribe called the Kansa. The word possibly means "People of the South Wind."

State Capital: Topeka, population 127,215

Date of Statehood: January 29, 1861 (34th state)

Population: 2,904,021 (34th-most populous state)

Area (Total Land and Water): 82,278 square miles (213,099 sq km), 15th-largest state

Largest City: Wichita, population 388,413

Nickname: The Sunflower State

Motto: *Ad Astra per Aspera* (To the Stars through Difficulties)

State Bird: Western Meadowlark

State Flower: Wild Sunflower

State Tree: Eastern Cottonwood

State Animal: American Bison

State Song: "Home on the Range"

Highest Point: Mount Sunflower, 4,039 feet (1,231 m)

Lowest Point: 679 feet (207 m) on the Verdigris River in Montgomery County

Average July High Temperature: 92°F (33°C)

Record High Temperature: 121°F (49°C), in Fredonia on July 18, 1936, and Alton on July 24, 1936

Average January Low Temperature: 19°F (-7°C)

Record Low Temperature: -40°F (-40°C), in Lebanon on February 13, 1905

Average Annual Precipitation: 28 inches (71 cm)

Number of U.S. Senators: 2

Number of U.S. Representatives: 4

U.S. Postal Service Abbreviation: KS

GEOGRAPHY

Kansas is a Great Plains state. It covers 82,278 square miles (213,099 sq km). It is the 15th-largest state.

The Missouri River makes up the northeastern border of Kansas. The Kansas River is also in the northeast. The Arkansas River (pronounced ar-KAN-sas by local people) runs through the western and southern parts of the state. Parts of the river dry out in summer.

Kansas appears to be flat, but it gently rises in the west. The lowest part of Kansas is 679 feet (207 m) above sea level on the Verdigris River, in the southeast. The highest point is a mound called Mount Sunflower, on the plains of the northwest. It is 4,039 feet (1,231 m) above sea level.

Kansas is filled with flat prairie lands and gently rolling hills.

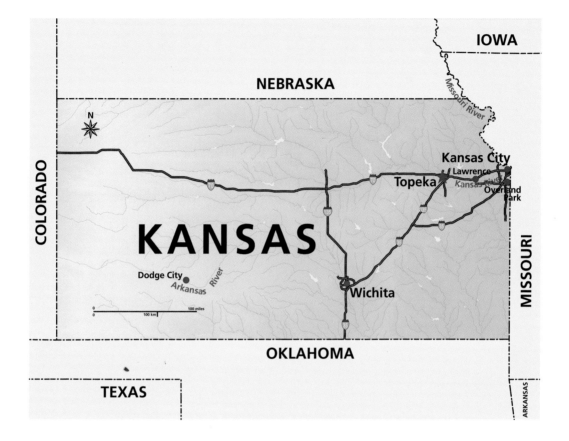

Kansas's total land and water area is 82,278 square miles (213,099 sq km). It is the 15th-largest state. The state capital is Topeka.

In the southeast corner of the state is the Ozark Plateau. It is hilly and wooded. The Red Hills of south-central Kansas get their name because of iron oxide (rust) within the soil. The Smoky Hills are in the north-central part of the state. They include rolling plains, gullies, and sandstone buttes.

The gently rolling Flint Hills occupy much of east-central Kansas. They include some of the largest tracts of unplowed tallgrass prairies in North America. The soil in the Flint Hills is too thin and rocky for farming.

The western part of Kansas is mostly wind-swept plains. There are few rivers or trees on this gently rolling landscape. It is called post rock country. Settlers once used limestone instead of scarce trees to build fences.

Mushroom Rock State Park is in the Smoky Hills Region of north-central Kansas. The 5-acre (2-ha) park features Dakota sandstone rock formations. Mushroom Rock is one of the most well-known hoodoos. It served as a landmark and meeting place for Native Americans and pioneers.

A dirt road divides two wheat fields in Grant County, Kansas. The field on the right benefits from irrigation courtesy of the Ogallala Aquifer that lies 600 feet (183 m) beneath. The field on the left is not irrigated. The wheat did not survive due to lack of rain.

The climate is dry on the western plains. But underneath the land is a hidden treasure: the Ogallala Aquifer. Located beneath Kansas and neighboring Great Plains states, this groundwater storage space holds more water than it would take to fill Lake Huron, one of the Great Lakes. Water is drawn from the aquifer to irrigate thirsty Kansas farm fields. However, more water is being withdrawn than goes into the aquifer through rain or other natural processes. Farmers are looking for ways to conserve water and use it more efficiently.

GEOGRAPHY

CLIMATE AND
WEATHER

Kansas has a continental climate, with warm summers and cold winters. There are few long stretches of temperature extremes. The growing season is long, from about mid-April to mid-September.

The eastern third of Kansas gets more rain, more humidity, and less sunshine than the western plains. The plains are at a higher altitude than the rest of the state. Also, they are in the "rain shadow" of the Rocky Mountains in neighboring Colorado. Eastward-moving clouds dump most of their rain over the mountains. By the time they float over western Kansas, they have little moisture. Statewide, Kansas receives 28 inches (71 cm) of precipitation yearly.

A Wichita, Kansas, family has fun after a heavy snowstorm.

A state trooper's car faces a bell-shaped tornado in Pretty Prairie, Kansas.

In winter, windy Kansas sometimes experiences blizzards, with blinding snow and freezing temperatures. In summer, severe thunderstorms often rumble overhead, sometimes bringing damaging hail. And, as anyone who has ever seen *The Wizard of Oz* knows, Kansas is in the heart of Tornado Alley. On average, Kansas is struck by 96 tornadoes each year. Most are small, but some are very destructive.

PLANTS AND
ANIMALS

Kansas prairies are filled with hundreds of species of grasses and flowering plants. There are more than 1,000 species in the Flint Hills region alone. Prairie grasses have long roots, which prevent soil erosion. They also provide food and shelter for animals. Some tallgrasses can reach heights of six to eight feet (1.8 to 2.4 m). Their deep roots help them survive the harsh weather conditions on the prairie.

Common grasses growing in the prairies of Kansas include big bluestem, little bluestem, Indian grass, switchgrass, buffalo grass, purpletop, prairie cordgrass, and Virginia wild rye.

In the spring and early summer, millions of wildflowers splash the Kansas countryside with color. They include fringe-leaf Ruellia, blue wild-indigo, wild alfalfa, cardinal flower, purple coneflower, butterfly milkweed, annual broomweed, and plains ragwort. The official state flower of Kansas is the wild sunflower. These beautiful yellow flowers are found throughout the state.

White-tailed deer look over ice-covered bluestem grass after a Kansas storm.

Many animals make their home in Kansas's fields, prairies, and forests. They include opossums, muskrats, jackrabbits, cottontail rabbits, foxes, squirrels, pocket mice, kangaroo rats, beavers, big brown bats, prairie dogs, moles, armadillos, porcupines, weasels, bobcats, mule deer, and white-tailed deer. Sometimes black bears wander into Kansas from neighboring states. The Kansas state animal is the American bison. Once, millions of these huge herbivores roamed the plains of Kansas. Today, a few captive herds can be seen scattered across the state.

Birds thrive in Kansas. The official state bird is the small western meadowlark. Its flutelike melody can often be heard ringing across Kansas farm fields. Other birds that make their home in Kansas include whooping cranes, bald eagles, falcons, blue jays, sparrows, owls, woodpeckers, cardinals, piping plovers, and greater prairie chickens (also called grouse).

A bald eagle sits in a cottonwood tree near Lawrence, Kansas.

There are about 5.2 million acres (2.1 million ha) of forest and woodlands in Kansas. That is about 10 percent of the state's land area. The most common tree is the eastern cottonwood. It is the official state tree of Kansas. Cottonwoods are often seen along the banks of rivers and streams. They are hardy trees, resistant to fire, drought, and flooding.

Other trees commonly seen in Kansas forests include hackberry, green ash, American elm, Osage orange, black walnut, bur oak, mulberry, American sycamore, and honey locust. There are no pine trees native to Kansas.

HISTORY

People have lived in today's Kansas for many thousands of years. Paleo-Indians were the ancestors of today's Native Americans. During the last Ice Age, they hunted big game such as mammoths and mastodons. By about 1,000 AD, some of these people added to their diet by growing crops, including squash and corn.

Around the time Europeans began exploring the North American continent, there were several Native American tribes living in Kansas. They included the Osage, Wichita, Pawnee, Arapaho, Kiowa, Comanche, Cheyenne, and Kansa tribes. The state is named after the Kansa people, who were also called the Kaw. Their name means "People of the South Wind."

In 1541, the first Europeans entered Kansas. They were from Spain. They were on an expedition led by Francisco Vásquez de Coronado. They left from Mexico searching for riches in the desert Southwest. In 1541, they made it as far as present-day central Kansas before turning back. They encountered many Native American tribes during the journey, but found no gold.

The Native Americans got something better than gold: horses left behind by the Spaniards. They learned to use them to hunt buffalo more effectively.

A statue of a Kansa, or Kaw, Native American stands in Council Grove, Kansas. Their name means "People of the South Wind."

For more than 100 years after Coronado's 1541 expedition, Europeans seldom ventured into Kansas. By the late 1600s, explorers from France claimed a huge part of North America, including Kansas. The French called their territory Louisiana. (Today's state of Louisiana was just a small part.)

Kansas became a part of the United States in 1803. President Thomas Jefferson bought Louisiana from France for just $15 million. It added approximately 828,000 square miles (2,144,510 sq km) of land to the country. The sale was called the Louisiana Purchase. The Lewis and Clark expedition arrived in the northeast corner of Kansas in 1804 as part of a mission to explore the new territory. Explorer Zebulon Pike crossed Kansas two years later.

Reenactors portraying Lewis and Clark fire a cannon on a replica keelboat on the Missouri River near Atchison, Kansas.

The town of Lawrence, Kansas, was attacked and burned by pro-slavery Confederate troops in August 1863.

Until 1854, Kansas was set aside as land for Native Americans. They included Native Americans from the East, whose land had been taken from them by white settlers. In 1854, most of the Native Americans were forced to move again, this time to Oklahoma in the south. White settlers poured into Kansas to farm the land.

Before the Civil War (1861-1865), new states had to choose whether to allow slavery or not. People from both sides rushed into Kansas. There were many deadly fights before anti-slavery forces finally won. Because of the conflict, the state became known as "Bleeding Kansas."

Farmers build a bonfire to try to repel a grasshopper plague in 1874. Millions of destructive locusts appeared as grey-green clouds that darkened the Kansas sky. The ravenous insects ate crops, trees, grass, clothing, leather, and wood. Cold weather finally killed them, but many settlers were left with nothing.

Kansas became a state on January 29, 1861. The Civil War (1861-1865) started within months. More than 20,000 Kansans fought on the side of the Union against the pro-slavery Confederacy. By the end of the war in 1865, more than 8,500 had been wounded or killed.

Early settlers had a tough time in western Kansas. They faced an arid land with few trees, frequent dust storms, Native American raids, and swarms of grasshoppers. Still, they found a way to thrive. Mennonite immigrants from Russia brought special wheat called Turkey Red. It grew well in the Kansas soil. Irrigation helped the crops grow.

Railroads began crisscrossing the Kansas landscape. In the 1860s and 1870s, cowboys from Texas rounded up huge herds of cattle and drove them north to Kansas towns along the railways. From there, the cattle could be moved by train to hungry cities in the East. Busy Kansas "cowtowns" included Dodge City, Abilene, Wichita, Caldwell, and Ellsworth. Many legendary lawmen of the Old West worked in cowtowns, including Wild Bill Hickok, Wyatt Earp, and Bat Masterson.

During the Great Depression of the 1930s, many Kansans lost their jobs. In addition, a long drought led to the Dust Bowl. During World War II (1939-1945), the economy grew again. Aircraft production greatly helped the Wichita area. Today, Kansas relies on manufacturing and service industries as well as agriculture.

A cowboy rounds up cattle on a Kansas ranch in 1902. Huge herds of cattle were driven to Kansas towns along the railways. From there, the animals were transported to cities in the East.

23

DID YOU KNOW?

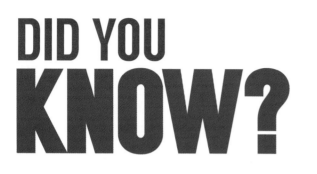

- Kansas is in the center of the contiguous United States (all the states except Hawaii and Alaska). The exact geographic center is in a farm field near Lebanon, Kansas. To protect the privacy of the landowner, a stone monument commemorates the spot about a half mile (.8 km) away in a small park. Because of its unique geographical position, Kansas is sometimes nicknamed "The Navel of the Nation."

- Monument Rocks in west-central Kansas are a series of chalk formations that rise up from the surrounding plains. They are the eroded remnants of an ancient sea floor that formed millions of years ago. Also called the Chalk Pyramids, the rock outcroppings are a National Natural Landmark. They are about 70 feet (21 m) high.

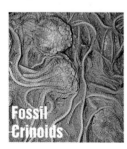

Fossil Crinoids

- Kansas was covered by an ancient inland sea millions of years ago. When the water finally drained, it left behind a mostly flat plain with rich, fertile soil. Today, some of the finest fossils of ancient fish and other sea life can be found in western Kansas.

- The Cheyenne Bottoms Wildlife Area is an important wetland for hundreds of thousands of migrating shorebirds. It is part of a 41,000-acre (16,592-ha) natural land sink in central Kansas, near the city of Great Bend. It is the largest wetland in the interior of the United States. Almost half of North America's shorebird species stop at the refuge during their spring migration. The birds like to feed on the clouds of insects that swarm in the marsh.

Prairie Rattlesnake

- There are 38 species of snakes commonly found in Kansas. Only a few are venomous. Timber rattlesnakes are found in eastern Kansas. Prairie rattlesnakes are common in the western plains. Both are about three to four feet (.9 to 1.2 m) long. The massasauga is smaller. It is sometimes called a "pygmy" rattler. It is often found in the prairies of the Flint Hills. Copperheads make their home in eastern Kansas. They like rocky ledges in woodlands. Like all snakes, these venomous reptiles are helpful to the state's ecosystems. They eat mice, voles, and rats. Although non-venomous snakes far outnumber venomous snakes in Kansas, hikers should take care when exploring. Look carefully before stepping over logs or climbing rocky ledges.

PEOPLE

Amelia Earhart (1897-1937) became the first woman pilot to fly solo across the Atlantic Ocean in 1928. Before her historic flight, she set many aviation speed and altitude records. Earhart was born in Atchison, Kansas, and spent her early childhood in the state. She learned to fly in her early 20s in California by working odd jobs to pay for lessons and buy her first plane. After her solo flight across the Atlantic Ocean, the United States Congress awarded her the Distinguished Flying Cross. She was very active in promoting equality for women, and even became friends with First Lady Eleanor Roosevelt. In 1937, Earhart tried to fly around the world. On July 2, 1937, she and her navigator, Fred Noonan, disappeared while over the Pacific Ocean. They were never seen again.

I LIKE IKE

Dwight Eisenhower (1890-1969) was the 34th president of the United States. He was born in Denison, Texas, but grew up in Abilene, Kansas. His nickname was "Ike." During World War II, Eisenhower was the supreme commander of Allied Forces in Europe. He led the fight against Nazi Germany, and rose to the rank of five-star general of the United States Army. He was diplomatic but tough. After the war, the popular Eisenhower was elected president. His campaign slogan was "I like Ike." Eisenhower served two terms, from 1953 to 1961.

Walter Johnson (1887-1946) was one of the greatest Major League Baseball pitchers to ever play the game. The right-hander started his career in 1907 playing for the Washington Senators. He pitched 21 years for the team, winning 417 games. His 110 shutouts is an all-time career record. Famous for his fastball, his nickname was "The Big Train." He was inducted into the National Baseball Hall of Fame in 1936. Johnson was born in Humboldt, Kansas.

Lucy Hobbs Taylor (1833-1910) was the first American woman to earn a doctorate degree in dentistry. Born in New York, she had trouble entering a dental school because she was a woman. She was accepted by the Ohio College of Dental Surgery and graduated in 1866. Dr. Taylor moved to Lawrence, Kansas, in 1867, where she was a respected dentist for more than 20 years.

Gordon Parks (1912-2006) was a photographer, film director, author, and musician. He was born in Fort Scott, Kansas. He taught himself photography in the 1930s. His work often showed proud and dignified African Americans during the civil rights era. Parks believed that photography could change people's minds about inequality and prejudice. His work was famously featured in *LIFE* magazine and the government's Farm Security Administration (FSA).

Joe Engle (1932-) is a pilot and former NASA astronaut. He served in the United States Air Force in the 1950s and 1960s. As a test pilot, he flew more than 185 kinds of aircraft, including the X-15. He started working for NASA in 1966. In 1981, he was the commander of STS-2, the second flight of space shuttle *Columbia*. Engle was born in Chapman, Kansas.

CITIES

Topeka is the capital of Kansas. Its population is 127,215. It lies along the Kansas River in the northeastern part of the state. Topeka is a Kansa-Osage Native American phrase that roughly means, "the place for digging potatoes." The impressive state capitol building was finished in 1903, after 37 years of construction. It was made of limestone dug from Kansas quarries. Besides government, other top Topeka employers include education, health care, and retail stores. Topeka is home to the Kansas Museum of History, the Combat Air Museum, and the Topeka Zoo.

Wichita is the largest city in Kansas. Its population is 388,413. It is in the south-central part of the state, along the Arkansas River. In the late 1800s, it was one of the busiest cowtowns in Kansas. Today, it is a center for aircraft manufacturing. Its nickname is "The Air Capital of the World." The Wichita Art Museum is the largest art museum in the state, with more than 8,000 pieces in its permanent collection. Wichita State University enrolls about 15,000 students in more than 60 undergraduate degree programs.

Kansas City's Legends Outlet is a popular shopping center with retail, dining, and entertainment.

Kansas City, Kansas, is the third-largest city in the state. It is a center for transportation, food processing, health care, medical research, and automobile assembly. The city is situated in the northeast part of the state, where the Missouri and Kansas Rivers meet. Across the Missouri River is the city's bigger neighbor, Kansas City, Missouri. Kansas City, Kansas, has a population of 149,636. However, the entire Kansas City metropolitan area is home to almost 2.4 million people. It combines the two Kansas City towns, plus other large suburbs such as Overland Park and Olathe. (Overland Park is Kansas's second-largest city, with a population of 184,525.)

Lawrence is in northeast Kansas, along the shores of the Kansas River. Its population is 92,763. In the 1800s, the city was the center of much violence during the "Bleeding Kansas" struggle over slavery. Today, Lawrence is a center for education, agriculture, and industry. It is home to many artists and musicians. The University of Kansas is the city's biggest employer.

Dodge City is in southwest Kansas. Its population is 28,117. It is a center for meatpacking, manufacturing, health care, and tourism. The city is most famous for its 1880s cowtown days. Today, the Boot Hill Museum features thousands of Old West weapons and artifacts, plus authentic living history demonstrations, including gunfight reenactments.

TRANSPORTATION

There are 140,687 miles (226,414 km) of public roadways in Kansas. There are many counties and small towns in Kansas, with roadways connecting them all. I-70 is an interstate highway that travels east and west through the middle of the state, from Kansas City in the east to the Colorado border in the west. In 1956, a section of I-70 west of Topeka became the very first part of the Interstate Highway System to be completed.

The Kansas Turnpike is a toll road that runs southwest and northeast. It connects Kansas City with Topeka, Emporia, and Wichita before ending at the Oklahoma border in the south. It was built in the mid-1950s, before the Interstate Highway System existed. Today, it includes sections of I-35, I-335, I-470, and I-70.

Kansas has 140,687 miles (226,414 km) of public roadways.

A coal train sits on the tracks in Syracuse, Kansas.

There are approximately 4,855 miles (7,813 km) of freight railroad tracks that crisscross Kansas. The most common bulk items hauled on Kansas railways include farm and food products, chemicals, petroleum products, and coal.

There are 367 public and private airports in Kansas. The state's biggest commercial airport is Wichita Dwight D. Eisenhower National Airport. It serves about 1.5 million passengers each year.

Wichita Dwight D. Eisenhower National Airport

NATURAL RESOURCES

Soil is the most important natural resource of Kansas. The official state soil is Harney silt loam. It is a dark brown prairie soil perfect for growing food crops. About 87 percent of Kansas is used to raise crops or as grazing for livestock. That is about 46 million acres (18.6 million ha) of land. There are approximately 61,000 farms in the state. The size of the average Kansas farm is 754 acres (305 ha).

Kansas is often ranked first in the nation for growing wheat and sorghum. It harvests an average of 328 million bushels of wheat annually. If Kansas farmers loaded a train with all the wheat they grew each year, it would stretch from the western part of the state all the way to the Atlantic Ocean. Kansas is also a leader in growing corn, soybeans, alfalfa, and hay. The state is well known for raising cattle and hogs.

Oil and natural gas used to be top Kansas mineral resources, but production has declined in recent years. The state is a major producer of lighter-than-air helium. Minor amounts of coal are mined in Kansas, but much more is imported from neighboring states. It is burned to generate electricity. Breezy Kansas gets about 19 percent of its electricity from renewable wind energy farms. Other Kansas mineral resources include limestone, gypsum, crushed stone, clay, and salt.

INDUSTRY

Kansas is often called "America's Breadbasket." However, even though most of Kansas is farmland, the majority of the state's citizens work in industries other than agriculture. These include transportation, utilities, retail trade, and the service industry. About 11 percent of the workforce is employed in manufacturing.

Kansans have been building airplanes since the 1910s, especially in the Wichita area. The state's wide-open spaces, lack of fog, central location, and good business climate all contributed to the aviation industry's success in the Sunflower State. Airplane manufacturing giants based in Wichita have included Cessna, Beechcraft, Bombardier Learjet, Boeing, Airbus, and Spirit AeroSystems. More than 32,000 people are employed in hundreds of Kansas aviation companies. More than a quarter of a million aircraft have been made in Kansas since 1919.

Business jets are assembled at a manufacturing plant in Wichita, Kansas.

Cars move across the assembly line at the General Motors Fairfax plant in Kansas City, Kansas.

Besides airplanes, Kansas factories build many other kinds of transportation equipment. They include automobiles, trucks, and railroad cars. Other manufactured goods include farm machinery, construction equipment, air-conditioning equipment, paints, tires, and camping gear.

Many Kansas companies make good use of the state's farm products. They include meatpacking plants and flour mills. Kansas food factories also process milk, cheese, baby food, bakery goods, and pet food.

SPORTS

There are no professional major league sports teams based in Kansas. Sporting Kansas City is a Major League Soccer (MLS) team based in Kansas City, Missouri. However, it plays its home games across the Missouri River in Kansas City, Kansas. Sporting Kansas City won the MLS Cup in 2000 and 2013. FC Kansas City is a women's professional soccer team based in Kansas City, Kansas. It plays home games in Kansas City, Missouri. The team won back-to-back championships in 2014 and 2015.

People in eastern Kansas are fans of Missouri teams such as the Kansas City Chiefs (football) and Kansas City Royals (baseball). In the western part of the state, there is big support for Colorado teams, especially the Denver Broncos (football).

There are several minor league sports teams in Kansas. They include the Kansas City T-Bones (baseball), the Wichita Wingnuts (baseball), and the Wichita Thunder (ice hockey).

The Kansas Speedway is in Kansas City, Kansas. It is a 1.5-mile (2.4-km) tri-oval track that hosts NASCAR races. The speedway can seat more than 72,000 race fans.

College sports are big in Kansas, especially football and basketball. The two most popular college teams are the University of Kansas Jayhawks from Lawrence, and the Kansas State University Wildcats from Manhattan, Kansas.

University of Kansas mascot Big Jay.

Kansas State mascot Willie Wildcat.

SPORTS

ENTERTAINMENT

The Kansas Museum of History is in Topeka. It has rare documents, plus exhibits about forts, trails, trains, African American history, the Civil War, and Kansas families.

The Natural History Museum at the University of Kansas in Lawrence includes four floors of exhibits. Visitors explore the natural world while learning about fossils, insects, snakes, birds, germs, and much more.

There are many blues and jazz clubs in Kansas City. Symphony orchestras can be found in Wichita and Topeka.

The Dwight D. Eisenhower Presidential Library and Museum is in Abilene. It includes many books, documents, and artifacts relating to the 34th president of the United States. President Eisenhower's grave and boyhood home are also on the site.

The Schlitterbahn Waterpark in Kansas City, Kansas, features tube slides, chutes, beaches, and lazy rivers. Verrückt is the world's tallest waterslide. Riders in a three-person inflatable raft plummet from a height of more than 168 feet (51 m).

Old Cowtown Museum in Wichita brings to life the pioneer history of Kansas. It is an open-air museum with living history exhibits. There are 54 historic and recreated buildings on the grounds, with more than 10,000 authentic objects from 1865-1880.

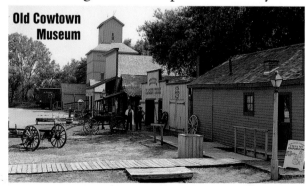

Old Cowtown Museum

Verrückt (German for "insane") is the tallest waterslide in the world. Riders climb 264 steps to the top and ride 168 feet 7 inches (51 m) to the bottom. Verrückt opened in 2014 at the Schlitterbahn Waterpark in Kansas City, Kansas.

TIMELINE

1541—Spanish explorer Francisco Vásquez de Coronado is the first European to travel through Kansas.

1682—French explorer René-Robert Cavelier, Sieur de La Salle claims the Kansas area for France.

1803—Kansas is included in the Louisiana Purchase, making it a part of the United States.

1855-1861—Kansans fight over whether the state will be a slave state or a free state.

1861—Kansas becomes the 34th state.

1954—The U.S. Supreme Court outlaws segregation in public schools in a case that started in Topeka, Kansas.

1966—The Topeka Tornado strikes on June 8. Rated an F5 (the most damaging kind of tornado), it injures more than 500 people and kills 17 others while causing more than $200 million in damage.

1980s—Kansas economy suffers because of low oil prices and farm failures.

1990s—Kansas economy improves, businesses expand.

2008—The University of Kansas men's basketball team wins the NCAA National Championship.

2014—Verrückt, the tallest raft waterslide in the world, opens at Schlitterbahn Waterpark in Kansas City, Kansas.

2015—The FC Kansas City NWSL women's professional soccer team wins the national championship for the second year in a row.

GLOSSARY

AVIATION

The flying or operating of airplanes.

DUST BOWL

A huge dust storm hits Elkhart, Kansas, in the 1930s.

In the 1930s, the Great Plains region of the United States, including the state of Kansas, was over-farmed and then had little rain for several years. High winds swept across the dry land, creating huge dust storms.

GREAT DEPRESSION

A time in American history beginning in 1929 and lasting for several years when many businesses failed and millions of people lost their jobs.

GREAT PLAINS

The land east of the Rocky Mountains, west of the Mississippi River and stretching from Canada to the Mexican Border. It is mostly covered with grass and few trees.

HOODOO

A rock that has weathered at different rates to form a tall spire shape with a harder rock top.

LEWIS AND CLARK EXPEDITION

An exploration of western North America, led by Meriwether Lewis and William Clark, from 1804-1806.

LIMESTONE

A hard rock used in buildings and in making lime and cement. Limestone forms over millions of years from the remains of shells, coral, and other marine life.

LOUISIANA PURCHASE

The purchase by the United States of about 828,000 square miles (2,144,510 sq km) of land from France in 1803.

MARSH

A type of wetland with lots of tall grass.

MENNONITES

A Christian group known for adult baptism and its refusal to fight in wars. In the 1870s, Mennonites from today's Germany who had moved to Russia eventually traveled to the United States and settled in Kansas. They brought with them Turkey Red wheat, which grew well in the Kansas prairie soil.

PLAIN

A large, flat area of land.

PRAIRIE

An ecosystem that includes grasses and flowering plants. Most of the plant roots are deep under the surface. It takes many years for prairies to form. Frequent fires burn off dead material and return nutrients to the soil. Deep-rooted plants then re-sprout. This cycle of death and regrowth forms rich, black soil over many thousands of years.

SORGHUM

A kind of grass used for livestock feed and to make ethanol fuel. People also use it to make flours, porridges, and side dishes. Some like to eat it as a popped grain, like popcorn.

TORNADO ALLEY

An area of the United States that has many tornadoes. Tornado Alley stretches from Texas in the south to North Dakota in the north and east to parts of Ohio.

INDEX